SistersRoc'N'Rhyme Solos-Part One

Unsung Canaan Ballads

I0521821

*A Collection of
Poems
by
Chyrel J. Jackson*

*Black Expression
Volume VII*

ISBN 978-1-962374-68-2 Paperback Edition
ISBN 978-1-962374-69-9 ePub

Library of Congress Control Number: 2025927035

Book Interior Design by: Usman Monday
Cover Design and Artwork/Cover By: Aleena Ali, Iqra Pervaiz & SistersRoc'N'Rhyme

All Graphic Images are Licensed or Public Domain

Dedication

This one's for my God, the poets, and the heartbroken.

May the words that live inside of you bring healing on their wings.

Table of Contents

Foreword

Unsung Canaan Ballads is a true collection of culture, pride, truth, family, history, emotion, and literary excellence.

I know I speak with some bias, after all, this is the woman I grew up always wanting to be, but I am so proud of her stepping out on her own and using her voice and words to give the world literary beauty, black culture and black history during a time when American leadership is doing everything in its power to silence, rewrite, and delete our history.

This work of poetry is a love letter to that we are as Black people living in a whitewashed world. "Open Your Eyes" is a powerful piece of truth, facts, and emotion. "Summer Memories of a Southern Bell Swinging", is a beautiful tribute to our beloved mother, whom I will never forget her swinging in the backyard on the swing that daddy built for her. "Food for the Soul" and "Harold's Chicken with a Side of Black Culture", is just that, Black food, Black culture, while celebrating Black life on the Southside of Chicago. Which truly brings back happy memories for me.

I remember the sweet days of sitting in Mommy's kitchen anticipating that bowel of red beans and rice with that side of buttermilk corn bread. What great childhood memories and it is because of that; I try to recreate those memories for my son. He was coming home from the military and before his plane landed, he texted me to have him some red beans and rice, with buttermilk corn bread. Needless to say, the crockpot was up and ready. I also remember bribing my older brother, Tony, over to my house by offering to buy him some Harold's Chicken if he came. It worked every time.

Chyrel is truly walking in the footsteps of our ancestors, picking up the baton to help us as a people continue to fight the battles we have fought since we landed in this Babylon. In the spirit of Fannie Lou Hamer, Ella Baker, Daisy Bates, and Mary McLeod Bethune, Chyrel calls attention to the Black struggle, with elegant words and rhythm, rocking in rhymes. And I'm truly proud to call her my sister.

With ever endearing pride, joy and love I say to my sister in the words of our Daddy, "Give'm Hell, Chyrel, give'm hell!

Lyris D. Wallace

Voices Echoed within the Wind

We are the pulse
The heartbeat of the
world
We are the rhythm of the
nations
Our beat is heard throughout
the earth
Our voices are echoed within
the winds
We drive, we pulsate, we are
rhythm and rhyme
Our stories we sing through space
and time
We are spirituals,
we're gospel, ragtime,
rock & roll
Bluegrass. country and everybody
knows we're the low down
dirty blues
Singing out truths
You can't erase it or replace it
You can't delete it or rewrite it
Because Moses already recorded it
And as long as the wind blows,
the sun shines and a child is born,
We're going to keep on telling it
We are the pulse
The heartbeat of the world
The rhythm of the nations
And our voices are echoed within the
winds

LDW

Acknowledgements

All family members and ancestors who no longer dwell on the earth.

Saying goodbye to Antoine, Edna Mae, Sylvester, and Elizabeth was an unimaginable heartbreak.

Time does not make their presence missed any less.

Writers, and their love of words and language. Our words never turn off. I am compelled to write them at the most bizarre moments of the day.

This seems strange, releasing poems without my sister on the side of me. She's with me here in spirit even now during this, my first solo writing effort. I love you, Chubbs, world without end.

Thank you for writing such a lovely foreword. It sets the perfect tone.

Lyris, you've always been there. I have loved you my whole life. Wherever I find myself, you are always home to me.

Michael, you're always cheering for me; I couldn't fly without you. You are my heart's greatest, last, and only love.

Jennifer, you have been a sunflower all your days. You pour so much love and light into this old soul of mine. Thank you for reminding me who I am.

Mama Barbara, if love were a person, it would be you.

The stone of Israel. Lord, I thank you for allowing the words to continue. There were days when my strength wasn't strong. This is quite special, and I don't take your mercy or grace for granted. Unsung Canaan Ballads is for you. Thank you, Father, in Jesus's name. Thank you for using an imperfect vessel for your glory.

The absolute best publisher in our industry, Lisa Tomey-Zonneveld. This wonderful human being is more than a publisher; she's my friend and soul sister.

Dr. Michael Anthony Ingram, I am honored to call you my friend.

Hezekiah Morris, my creative brother who always reminds me who I am. He's always in these streets making the impossible possible. Hez, thank you for letting me know what is possible.

Juntu Ahjee, wherever life takes me, I promise I'll always create a space somewhere for you too.

Carlos (C.T.) Miller and all Black writers who allowed me to see what was possible. I will love you beyond the kingdom of God.

Thank you to Zan, Artemis, and Anjie, women whom push me forward and make me a better sister.

Especially James Baldwin, who first passed me the torch.

Author's Note:

For better or worse, I am my parents' daughter. All that they loved, I love too. Books, art, nature, and music have enriched my life in profound ways I can't verbalize. Living life without them has been quite difficult.

The pain of writing hasn't been as joyful with their absence. I miss telling them about the latest book I'm reading. I wonder what they would think about the books I have written.

Unsung Canaan Ballads blends the essence of my existence up to this juncture. It is just as the title suggests, an Uncelebrated-Unsung Canaan-Promised Land book of Poems-Ballads.

Unsung Canaan Ballads is a walk-through of scenes from a Black Life!

It's my first solo effort alone without Lyris. She's my strong tower and voice of okay. I look to her to help me make sense of what is difficult to understand. I look to and count on her support.

Unsung Canaan Ballads is history, poetry, music, and a daughter's loving tribute to the parents that she loved more than anything in the world.

I once wrote words that, when released into the universe, provide healing. I hope someone discovers some for that hurting soul during a time of unbelievable loss.

Books, music, and writing all help me coexist in a world that is quite overwhelming. These are my escape mechanisms.

I hope something stirs a loving memory within you from something that I have written. I hope you see something a little different from your first glance.

History is being rewritten, erased; books banned by those that want to stamp out the truth. I can't pretend that these things aren't happening. They are.

It is my job to write about life as it is happening in real time. My parenting, mirroring predecessors, embodied history. Unsung Canaan Ballads is my tribute to their unique and courageous legacy.

Here's to building my own. May the person hurting, hoping to find themselves, find healing, escape, and comfort in the words within this volume of poems.

You will emerge from the dark times, and you will find joy in life's music again.

The one constant through-line in life music heals. My parents understood that. I'm learning that most poignant lesson now.

cjj

Chapter One

"We hung our harps Upon the willows in the midst thereof."

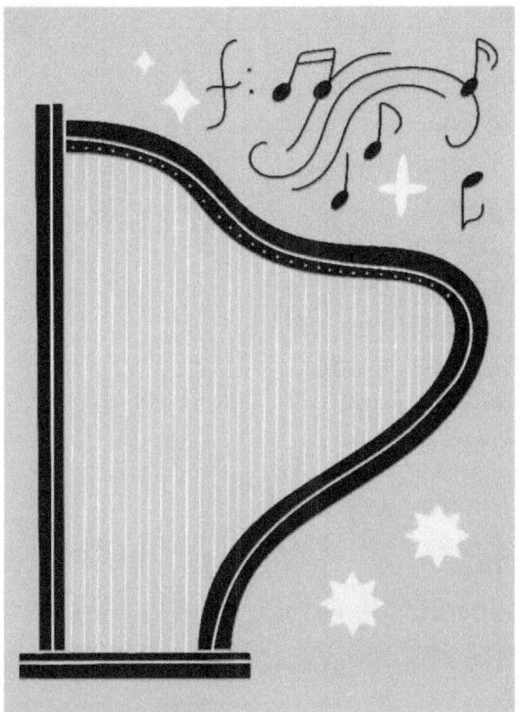

"How shall we sing the Lord's song in a strange land?"

Weeping Willow

Can you imagine hurt so
acute that all of life's
simple pleasures disappear?
Music no longer sung.
The familiar tunes suddenly
stop.
Your feet no longer dance.

They can't remember movement.
The radio has become
covered in cobwebs and dust
from lack of use.
I remember a story in the
Bible where the children
of Israel were so depressed
they hung their harps upon
trees; they were not able
to play them anymore.

Weeping Willow weep for me.

That's how I feel.
Life has swallowed me whole.

Nothing left, not even skeletal

remains of my beaten down soul.
There isn't any music left in me.
Loved one's dead and gone.
What remains we are now estranged.
The guilty remain unnamed.

Everything broken

Everything strange.

Forever changed.

No longer the same.
I can't hum, sing, or dance.
This is my season of sorrow.
My heart remembers music,
song, dancing, and joy.
Why can't I be at that place
anymore?
I remember the music.
At this point, sadness
pervades.
The PTSD of living has taken
over.
I hum the negro spirituals to
feel closer to my mother.
I hum a sorrowful chorus of
the Egyptians being swallowed
up in the Red Sea.
Weeping Willow weep for me.

I'm lonely and afraid there is
No Moses to deliver me.

I have hung my harp and
instruments of music upon the
highest tree.

cjj

Americana was My Grandmother's Glory

A needle and thread.

A needle and crochet needles.

A ballot.

Sewing American Democracy together one stitch and vote

at a time since our grandmother's and Grace Wisher.

One silent stitch at a time.

Americana doesn't see us.

We're the silent seamstress holding on to hope and covering

ourselves in our grandmother's glory.

We vote because our grandmothers couldn't.

We believe in purple mountain majesties and vote for American Democracy.

You will find us from sea to shining sea standing nobly above fruited plains.

Even when we're uncelebrated and unacknowledged.

Even when no one sees me.

I'm there cloaked in belief wearing deferred dreams as a banner yet waved.

I'm the 92 percent of Black womanhood that voted for a first ever Black woman president.

Still holding needle and thread in our weary hands.

Still stitching the red, white, and blue together all over the land.

Unseen holding on to hope, Black women believe in a system of government

that never embraced us back.

We are our grandmother's glory.

Were it not for Black women in America there wouldn't be an American story.

cjj

Reclaiming Country Roots

COUNTRY
Generations upon generations
of southern roots.
So, the blood from my
people enriched the soil and
stained many trees.

Country long before, my tis of thee.
My music bellowed loudly and
sounded on the wind as it
echoed from the southern
plantations of cotton and rice

fields.
White fragility and greed would
not allow them to crop and plant
their own yields.
They enslaved, purchased and sold

my people to do their work.

COUNTRY

My People survived they made
it through what most couldn't.
Overseers, mutilation, chains,
and whips.
My God, transatlantic Slave ships.
All with our instruments and songs
in our hearts.

COUNTRY

Creating low country, bluegrass

tunes.
Strumming our banjos, and fiddles.
Singing our negro spirituals and blues.
Country and unashamed.
Not in a fashion style.

Not in a highjacked name.

A way of life.
Country was never yours to claim.
Survivors called lazy after being

overworked Sunup to Sundown.
Even survived your racist Sundown towns.

COUNTRY

Pick your Massacre as recorded in
History.
Memphis, Atlanta, Tulsa, and
Rosewood.
Descendants of Black people that
survived the brutality of Ocoee,
and Charleston would all agree.

A sunburnt Black, melanated people

from the south and southwestern roots.

COUNTRY

A blending of Black music genres.

We are the origins of Blues, Gospel,

Bluegrass and Folklore.

Playing our instruments with music from

our soul given by God not centered in hate.

COUNTRY

The thing about country you can't

appropriate.

If it didn't begin with Black, it simply ain't

great.

COUNTRY

If country music not Black, then there

is no country music.

We are the sun burnt people from the

lowlands.

Cowboy Carter is a milestone and

musical marker of our contributions in all music

genres.

Makes our presence in Country known.

Those who co-opted a genre twisted up

with anger.

I smile broadly, you may lie for a time but
truth always prevails. History is recorded.
This brilliant music release is a retelling
and reclaiming of our eclectic musical
History. It is History. We are history.
My feet remember dancing.
My hands remember clapping.
I applaud elder generations' storytelling,
the fusion and blending of multiple
music genres.
I listen to Cowboy Carter and I
proudly embrace my southern sharecropper,
daughter of a Bluesman, roots.
COUNTRY

    Reimagined

    Reclaimed

COUNTRY is a melanated, sun burnt, Black
people from the lowlands who carry the
music of our God within our hearts.

cjj

Self-Reflection

Black Literature saw two little
Black girls.
It defined our lives.
Narratives of Black families
Church, and community.
Positive messages be all that
you can be.
Descriptive, engaging, written
how we sometimes speak it.
Celebrating Black life, culture
and majestic banners of our
Civic, civil, historical and moral
conscience.
Black Literature is the mirror
that casts back our very own
self-reflections.
Allowing us to embrace perfect
imperfections.
We can never repay our literary
heroes:
Hughes, Hurston, Angelou,
Baldwin, Sanchez, Giovanni,
Brooks, Shangé, Clifton and
others who simply rocked our
World.
Black Literature saw and saved
two little unseen exceptional
Black girls.

cjj

Goodnight Nikki

I looked into the sky as
sparkled half silver dollar sized
raindrops fell.
The scent of fresh rainwater
mixed with earth made my
senses tingle.
With my head pointed upwards
to the heavens daylight became
Winter's evening silent prayer.
The still and dark sky dried up
the sparkly afternoon rains.
Glittering stars resembling
confetti now splatter the cosmos.
Eventide bids me Goodnight.
I'm certain I see the familiar outline
of your knowing freckled face
shadowing a spellbinding dusky
full moon.
Goodnight Nikki and Goodbye.

cjj

Walking as Servants

God's people walk among us.
Unknown, unsung, under-appreciated
Many say unsophisticated.
Undervalued human cargo packed in
on transatlantic slave ships.
Known by our smiles despite the pain
of living extraordinarily significant lives.
Look at us glide, dance, sing, and fly.
God's people can do anything.
Everything he is, is within us.
We are the essence of his glory.
We are glorious.
Best athletes, inventors, scientists, too.
We are the rhythm within the music.
We write the psalms and live the proverbs.
We are the blues.
Walking the earth in walking shoes.
We are a royal priesthood.

Judah, Benjamin, and Levi

    walk upon the earth.

Undervalued human cargo least within the earth.
I declare, I have seen servants upon horses,

and princes walking as servants upon

    the earth.

cjj

The Roots

You lie about history
to diminish our roots.
We bear the hateful
scars of your brutal
physical and mental
tattoos.
The facts are always
there.
The records are stored
when not hidden,
everywhere.
Our ancestors paved the
way.
Shackled, beaten, maimed
and bruised.
They have spoken for a
long time.
In the still and quiet the
ancestors speak can you
hear them?

They are the life roots of

every tree that ever bear

grain.

From Timbuktu, and

every isle beyond the

Red Sea: I am

part of their supreme

lineage.

With time and chance

the awesome gifts of the

ancestors, make us one.

In the end of life's journey

the ancestors eventually

become me.

cjj

Blooming from Concrete

Tried, tested, misused,
used, then left for dead.
SistersRoc'N'Rhyme has had
more lives than the charmed
nine.
Cloaked in resilience with
hope, and faith we thrive.
We survived.
Tears in our eyes we
continue to try.
Two by Two side by side.
Despite difficulties and many
adversities the roses formed.
As the sun burned bright
we weathered the furnace of
life's often afflictions.
Suddenly we stood tall bursting
through the unyielding concrete.
Seeking the light.

Surviving the night.
Watch our Creator turn the turbulent
tides of life.
Two beautiful roses bloom side by side.
From the cement standing strong,
standing tall, no one ever expected
to see the unimaginable,

Two super industrial sized roses
splitting open implacable concrete.

cjj

She is Resilience

She has withstood it all.
Misogyny,
Patriarchy,
Sexism,
The Good Ole Boys.
Nothing could keep her
down.
She is durable.
Flexible,
Strong,
Tough,
Pliable,
Capable,
Tried and Tested.
Determined,
Adapt,
Constant,
Resolute.
Weathered and worn.
She is the fairer sex but never
the weaker sex.
Battle tested.
Purposed, Determined,
Tenacious, Persistent,
Sometimes bowed, yet unbroken.
Womanhood defined.
Resilience, Spoken.

cjj

Unmuted

She made us rise as we were
told why the caged bird sings.
We saw Black women poets
honored by Presidents.
As we watched the esteemed
poet honor 2 presidents.
Clinton then Obama.
Reciting poetry at 2 presidential
inaugurations.
History in the making.
Teacher, mother, sister and friend.
Her wisdom speaking still.
She saw us, when no one else did.
She spoke our language and
validated us.

Our muted voices boomed with

sound.
There wasn't a more phenomenal
voice for Black women.
The epitome of Black womanhood.
How many lessons we learned.
I stood taller as she said, I have my
own back.
Love is not binding it's freeing.
Maya Angelou freed Black women
giving us permission to love ourselves.
Believe what our eyes show us and
our hearts tell us the very first time.
Speak out loudly for yourselves.

The world can't hear a muted voice.
When they tell you, you can't.
Show them you will and can.
Even in fear, doubt, and in a
whisper find your voice within
you.

Tell the world plainly I am
God's child his power is within me.
Thank you for helping many
generations of women to find and

use our voice.

cjj

Joy

Joy is sun drenched rays pouring
through opened windows.
It's looking up in a never ending
dark sky at night and not being able
to count the infinite Constellations.
Joy is the smell of new born
babies and the hero worship of
being a cat mom and dog dad.
Our animals feel tremendous joy
when we award them with treats of
pup & kitty cups.
Dog Bones, and cat temptations.
Joy is watching a toddler successfully
take then master their very first steps.
Joy is your heart's greatest love loving
you back.
It's the way a daughter's dad
looks at her on her wedding day.
The gentle smile he gives her taking her
hand letting her know everything's going
to be okay.
Joy is what most people feel
at a dinner table with good
food there to eat.
Joy is breathing in the scents
of home in peace before I drift off
to sleep.
Joy in nature, sky, trees, and life.
Joy in the arms that, hold you tight.
Taking a breath breathing it in

Joy in the seasons, summer, fall,
winter and spring.
Joy in health, living, and grateful
for everything.

cjj

Chapter Two

"By the rivers of Babylon, there we sat down, yea, we wept, when we remembered Zion."

Instruments on Trees

A rebellious, unrepentant people.

Even our God likened us to wicked

and evil.

He turned his back on us.

No longer wanted to be among us.

He returned to his high place just

Look at our end.

Stacked up in slave ships like planks.

Took away everything even our

musical instruments.

God didn't even want to hear us sing.

Said our songs were noise to his

ears then placed us in captivity

for many years.

You know you're in trouble when God

declares he won't hear the melody of

our viols.

Driven from our homeland captive in

a strange land.

Longing to get back to the land of milk

and honey our beloved promised land.

Oh, Canaan Land my soul remembers

and longs for thee.

Remember our place and time

of love with you;

before we were captives

before the middle passage

before we learned to sing a new

song-My Country Tis of thee,

before our viols/harps and instruments

of music were hung on trees.

cjj

History Can't Be Rewritten

You cannot rewrite history.
I simply won't let you do that.
You won't pretend the last time
I saw you, you weren't unkind.
You won't behave now that
I'm gone like you weren't short,
abrupt, and didn't make time.
I will not allow you to sit here
In the open to pacify your guilt
and make believe that you cared
about me.
The last time I saw you, you
were terse and didn't have time.
I was there and I experienced all of
the real you.
Don't send greetings of grief
and bereavement to my loved
ones.
Please maintain the distance you
Seamlessly established before my
timely demise.
You cannot rewrite history.
I, nor my loved ones have any
interest in massaging your guilt.
We all saw and experienced the
real you.

You cannot erase or rewrite your
reckless and callous behavior the
last time I saw you.

cjj

Words You Can't Unsay

Tossing turning awake in my bed
Thinking of my failings
Sounding loudly rewinding
in technicolor living in my head.
Many gifts God lent me but
nothing of my own.
Lost everything that mattered
All I loved now gone.
Tony, mommy, daddy,
placed in the heart of the earth.
Living midlife years what is a
Black life worth?
Cared for many people, that
didn't care for me.
Kicked me while I was down
You can't live here for free.
I am wide awake now, sleep
is long gone.
Everyone I ever loved left me
It's clear I'm on my own.
Thinking of my failings
living in my head, hurtful
words from the demented
on rewind words that
cannot now be Unsaid.

cjj

Suffering in Silence

The quiet, awkward, and
sometimes disheveled
little girl or boy can't say
my uncle/dad touches
me in private places they
shouldn't.
Suffering in Silence
The kid that never has
lunch money won't ever say
I'm hungry.
They're too ashamed.
Suffering in Silence
The withdrawn teenager that
always falls to sleep in English
or Math class; won't admit their
family lives in a car and they were
evicted. Mom could no longer
afford the rent.
Suffering in Silence
Everyday human beings
fight wars within themselves
no one knows anything about.
Kindness costs nothing.
Pay attention pain is tangible
too many among us *suffering in
silence.*
Open your eyes come out of
yourself and notice the
words the people around you
in the most pain never say out
LOUD.   cjj

Black Parent's Talking Points

Talking to our children for

70 years since the murder

of Emmett Till.

Careful son driving while Black.

Stay alert daughter,

remain watchful while Black,

we tell our kids.

Pay attention.

Stay WOKE.

Keep your hands in front of

you at all times.

Their lives are in jeopardy.

Every day they leave our sight.

Their lives are in peril all

their days.

No listening to loud music,

No walking,

No jogging,

No sleeping,

No shopping,

No grabbing coffee at Starbucks

while Black.

Now add No ringing an unknown

doorbell while Black to our revised

Black parental talking points.

Black parents talking.

70-long years of talking.

Black parents crying.

Black parents in agony as we watch

Our Black children dying.

cjj

AJ Owens, Rodney King, Trayvon Martin, Jordan Davis, Tamir Rice, Oscar Grant, Ahmaud Arbery, Siyonbola, Daunte Wright, John Crawford, Rashon Nelson, Donte Robinson, Eric Garner, Breonna Taylor, George Floyd, Elijah Jovan McClain, Tyre Nichols, Philando Castille, Rayshard Brooks, Michael Brown, Laquan McDonald, and so many of our children without number.

Thanking God for sparing Ralph Yarl's 16-year-old life.

Ezra's Wall

My Ancestors built the ancient
places.
The walls and castles that
housed and held queens and
kings.
They fortified the broad walls.
The valley gate, and even
Ephraim's gate.

The locks with
the doors.
My people built the walls of
the pool by the king's garden.
The fields at Azekah and the
villages of Lachish.
Why does it matter who did
the building?

It is our sacred history and
rites of passage.
I know the history and assert
boldly someone is committing
identity theft.
They're not who they claim to be.
That someone isn't my Ancestors.
That someone isn't me.

My people built the stairs and walls
of the City of David.
Ezra stood by with sword in hand
as the people built.

The walls went up beyond the tower
of the furnaces.

History speaks loudly.
I assert louder still,
I KNOW THE HISTORY!

cjj

Food for the Soul

Red beans and Rice
isn't just soul food.
It is a delicacy, a delight
something southerners
fully understand.
It is a retelling of history,
a reliving and celebration
of culture and family.
It is Black southern legacy.
Red beans and Rice
is a mother's, aunt's and
grandmother's love.
Low country geechee roots.
Stomachs rumble in anticipation.
Prepared with care.
Seasoned to perfection.
Slow cooked with smoked turkey
bits.
The aromas cling in the air for
many hours long after consumed.
It's a gathering of family and friends.
Red beans and rice is a certainty
that all fortunate enough to gather
around the table will receive so much
more than great food.
It is loving familial bonds.
Red Beans and rice smells, feels, and

tastes like Home.

                    cjj

Estranged

The heaviest footfalls my heart
would ever know came from
family members lined up in
anger at my parents' front

door.
The loud crescendo of rushing
mendacious feet.
Such a dreadful, pitifully sad
day.

Where life becomes frozen in

time.

No strength to say what needs

to be said.

Out of respect for the newly
dead.

Stifling gasping cries.

Saying last goodbyes to everyone
that made me who I am.
Betrayal once seen and felt can't

be unseen.

When you were needed most you

did the least.

Robbers' housebreakers of my

peace.

All these years later those indignant
heavy footsteps that landed on the
front porch, took with them familiar
faces, childhood memories, traditions
and family history my heart wants so
much to forget.

I can hear vividly the betrayal of those

riotous feet.

Wishing I was anywhere else.
Estrangement comes at a heavy and
piteous cost.

Goodbye.
This time, I must save myself.

cjj

Harold's Chicken with a Side of Black Culture

Black urban dwelling
spaces have been defined
as ghetto tenement slums.
City front stoop brownstones
and high-rise apartment buildings.
Martin Luther King Avenue,
South, North and West sides
of the block.
Bright and beautiful Metropolis
Landscapes.
Breathtaking skylines
Nothing says City girl quite like
shopping on the Mag Mile.
The best food, music, art,
people, and culture are created
within these confines.
We like our tea, lemonade, and
beverages sweet.
Our orders of Harold's fried
chicken with salt and pepper,
mild sauce on the side; and an
extra helping of Mama's peach
cobbler/caramel cake to go.
If you know, then you know!

cjj

A Joyous People

The joy is in the
music, and the songs that

Black people sanggg.
how we worship our

God in church and

bang our tambourines.

The joy is in the
food we prepare.
The fish that we fry
and fried chicken
too.
Our cobblers and
cakes, the buttery
cornbread and
tender beef potatoes
and carrots with gravy
stew.
The music that we
create.
The naughty of Southern
Black Blues.
It's the written stanzas
of the poet's pen
and the preachers preachin'
gospels good news.
The joy is in our happy
hands clappin' and
soulful fingers snappin'.
The Bojangles of our
gleeful feet jiggin', dancin'
and Tappin'.

The cadence in our rap
songs that have the whole
world rappin'
These wondrous Black
People sing.
We smile.
We overcome
incredible odds set against
us.
Speaking out of injustice
that does not favor us.
Joy is in the culture of
the shared stories and
history we tell.
The happy within our
hearts that was never yours
to sell.
God's people are a joyous
People.
A talented and heartful

people.
Nothing like us in all the

earth.

The joy is in the
music, and the songs that

Black people sanggg.
how we worship our God

In church and bang our
tambourines.

Yeah, we are Men, women
and children most wondered
at and we be a real baadddd
and joyous people.

cjj

Chapter Three
Psalms at Sunrise

"Take thou away from me the noise of thy songs; for I will not hear the melody of the viols."

I Am...

I am worthy of all good things.
I am likeable.
I am witty.
I am intelligent.
I am a lover of nature.
I am kind.
I am strong.
I am a Scribe, I write.
I am History walking.

I am life.
I am the psalms of
King David talking.
A teller of truth.

I am all this and so much more.
I am an animal rights advocate.
I am a nurturer.
I am a wanderer.
I am a wonder.

I am successful.
I can do and be anything.
I am called many things.
I am capable of anything.
Despite stereotypes, unkind words,
and labels placed on me; from others.
I am what God says I am; and

always will be.
Like God, who came before me.
Was, and forever more will be.

I am life,

I am comfort,

I am wisdom

I am wife.

I am daughter

I am sunrise.

I am mother and

Resister.

I am respect

I am strength

I am lineage

And giver.

I am moonlight

I am time

I am the essence

Of life's river.

I am protector.

I am prayer warrior

I am faith

I am mercy

I am grace.

I am friend

I am love

I'm as endless as

the constellations

in the skies above.

I am legacy

I am history

Woman is the name

Father Adam first called me.

I am the heavens and

Earth's greatest mystery.

Like God, who came before

me was, and forever more

will be.

Long after I am gone.
as he, first was

Who came before me

days without number

and after me

I AM.

cjj

Summer Memories of A Southern Bell Swinging

Behind that sweet
mysterious smile
and such mischievous
eyes was the woman
we called mommy
patient and wise.
Benevolence was her
first and second nature.
I conjure up memories
of our warm, southern
bell swinging from her swing
outside.
This dear lady shaped
and influenced so many
lives.
I think of her daily reading
her Bible and History books.
A woman born out of
time.
Everything she did
Edna Mae did it well.
She packed so much
inside 67 years of
living.
Humor, memories,
and daughters
that immortalize
their lovely southern bell.
This beautiful being
gave me life.
Mommy is the reason
my sister and I write.

There's not a day in
summer where colorful
tiny birds sprout wings
I don't remember mommy
in the yard upon her
beautiful swing.
Swinging away looking
up into a summer sky;
memories of
our gentle southern bell
ever so patient and kind.
Mommy is what we
called her, a rare and lovely
                woman born out of Time.

                    cjj

Warriors, Musicians, and Kings

Uprooted

Traveled across thousands of miles

Survived the middle passage then

southern Cotton fields that baked

and burnt our Black skin.

We conquered the sun.

Jim Crow

subjugation

my people overcome.

We've forgotten our God.

Forgotten our purpose.

Music,

Culture,

History mostly all lost forgotten.

I remember who we used to be.

Before the siege.

Before the slave ships.

Before we hung our harps upon trees.

Black so much more than a color.

Still overcoming forgotten memories.

I remember when Blacks loved one another.

I remember the 12 tribes.

I remember Canaan land.

The royal priestly garments are difficult to forget.

Long before we were called the flock of the slaughter.

I remember our time of love.

Though it was only for a moment,

I remember our splendor.

The days of our rejoicing upon King Solomon's porch.

Before we were scattered

Before we were sold.

The throne our king once sat upon

Ivory and pure gold.

I remember our time of love.

Love of Black Culture,

Black unity.

We were and are Black History.

Loving one another.

So very long ago.

Our harps were not hung upon

trees then.

The slave ships couldn't break us

Oppression didn't stop us.

When we were one nation, I have

vivid memories of how the whole

World envied us.

Once upon a time, a very long time

ago we were warriors, musicians, priests,

and kings.

cjj

Lift Her Up

She is the beginning
and end of time.
Everything in between
Clouds and sunshine.
She is rain, wind, earth,
and fire.
Every human emotion
and desire.
She is love, courage,
and moral fortitude.
She is strength, wisdom,
blues, and bad attitude.
She is beauty and resilience.
Lift her up, Lift **her** up.
Stop demeaning,
degrading, and devaluing,
Black womanhood.
Lift her **up**, lift her up.
As she has always carried
and lifted up this morally
bankrupt nation.
Birthed its children,
nourished them, and
stood at the side of this
Black man; when the world
turned its back and dared
to look away.
For all these reasons and
more...
Lift her up, Lift her up,
LIFT HER UP, I say!!!!   cjj

Open Your Eyes

What Police Don't See
Athletes
Musicians
Poets
Teachers
Mothers
Fathers
Daughters
Sons
Brothers
Grandsons
Nephews
Aunts
Uncles
Children
Teenagers
Mental fragility
Black humanity
Female femininity
Male masculinity
Fear
Distress
Anxiety
PTSD
Resilience
Fatherhood
Motherhood
What Police take away
Aspirations
Matriarchs
Patriarchs
Breadwinners
Providers

Family
Hopes & Dreams
Holidays
Future
Birthdays
Tomorrow
Until you see me, you won't
serve and protect me.
Won't you consider seeing
me, before you kill me?

cjj

Betrayal

What if my roots went back
further than those of the
middle passage and
transatlantic Slave ships?
What if my DNA were traced
directly to my mother, Eve?
What if I could link back my
genetics to the olive trees and
Red Sea?
What if God talked directly
to his people before our
parents covered themselves
with leaves?
What if God's people looked
just like me?
Wooley, hair, skin, the color of
burned brass?
What if God's people were the
people that the world abused?
Lynched, shot, burned, and spit on?

People called colored, spades,

bywords, and spooks.

What if God hid all the history

of his people inside a binder of

books?

What if God's people were darker

than the darkest berry, kissed by

the sun?

Human cargo placed on Slave ships,

Sold as bond women and men.

What if God punished his people

because we first betrayed him?

What if the bloodshed poured

upon Black people was because

we dared say, let his blood be upon us?

The time we first chose the murdering

rebel named Barabbas?

                              cjj

Surpassing Lost Lullabies

Hope springs eternal...

I am the hope of my mother

and her mother's, mother.

I am tenacious

I am perseverance

I am lullabies sung and long

forgotten by way of the African

Nile.

I was born a Black girl grew into

Black womanhood.

I am a thousand generations

of stories waiting to be born and

told.

I am History walking.

I breathe, and write so that future

generations of Black girls after me

would live loud

fearlessly.

No hiding in the shadows

No shrinking themselves

Smaller.

Transcending mother's

fragile dreams of deferred,

yet to be, fulfilled hope.

I am made eternally optimistic

with mother's and great

grandmother's infinite expectation

of what is and can be possible.

Blackbird spread your wings and

flyyyyyy.

Soar beyond the northern skyyyyyy.

                              cjj

Humility

Art
Creation
Nature
Love
Great Music
Sisterhood
Mathematics
Change of Seasons
Dogs & Cats
Sunrises
Sunsets
Parents
Children
Amazing books
History
Literature
Science
Constellations
All make the human heart full,
and better.
Only a perfect being greater than
us; God, can create all this
majesty.
In my infinite fragility, I'm uncertain
of many things.
What I am most certain of is the
humility
felt beholding the magnificence of
God's majestic earthly landscape.
Birds singing
Sprawling Trees

Rainbows and waterfalls
Falling rain & falling stars
Flowers blooming in my front
and back yard;
Taking all this in makes me humble.
Makes me smaller.
I am certain there is no entity greater
than God.

cjj

All My Parts

These are all the pieces of me.
Mr. Calhoun's plantation.
Dad selling moonshine and
Old Mississippi dirt roads.
Emerald Avenue and Pheasant Lane.
I am the daughter of sharecroppers.
I fight to forget our parents' pain.
Dad left the dirty south and became
an architectural engineer because
North was where he could live life like
a man.
Despite the racism of our federal
government and surviving the degradation
of Jim Crow.
These are my pieces the pieces of fight
for your peace.
Write from your soul.
Fight Shelly there is no one better than you.
I fight to preserve Black Literature, Black

book bans and whitewashed Black
History too.
I fight to remember the part of it that
says I am the children of Israel long
before slavery and transatlantic Slave
ships declare who it is I'm supposed to be.
These are my pieces.
The pieces I fight to hold on to.
My pieces, the delicate pieces of me.
I write to remember my intricately
assembled and interwoven pieces.

The pieces of me, my life, lineage,
blood lines, music and songs.

I fight to hold on to dreams of

Canaan Land, Black history.

The only History that I've ever been
taught; 1619 Slavery.
I fight to hold on to and remember

all of my parts the pieces of me.

cjj

Untethered Bloodlines

Same parents
Same bloodlines
DNA and family
Structure.
Same face.
Same house.
Same residence.
Emerald Avenue and
Pheasant Lane.
Same siblings.
Same lineage.
Same background.
Same Culture.
Same upbringing.
Same history.
Same family recipes.
Same family secrets.
Same grandparents.
Same memories.
Same shared experience.
Same church.
Same God.
Same neighborhoods.
Same high-school.
Same neighbors.
Same struggles.
Same opportunities.
Different choices.

Different morals.
Different paths.
Different faith.
Different hope,
Different you.

cjj

Chapter Four
Eveningtide Selah

"That chant to the sound of the viol, and invent to themselves instruments of music, like David."

Blue Demons

Life has all of us in a chokehold.

We're all one step away from

mental breakdown.

Neurotic overload.

Exhaustion.

Anxiety.

Unrest.

Sometimes it's all just too much.

The daily news.

The job.

The bills.

Fighting to stay afloat.

Fighting with strangers.

Fighting with loved ones.

Isolation.

Alone in your home late.

It's the wee early morning hour.

You hear sounds banging on the

side of your house.

Fear appears you call for help.

Satan's minions show up instead.

Even in mental fragility and fatigue,

there's no mistaking this officer's

spirit just isn't right.

The officer won't leave

further engages,

you bid him goodnight.

He asks you to remove a pot from

the stove.

You obediently do so.

More exchange of words.

What happens next is deadly.

Newsflash to a hateful, rage filled

World.

I rebuke you in the name of Jesus.

Shots fired.

My God, we're all Sonya Massey.

cjj

A Little Bit Country

Grief is all consuming.
It takes so much away
from us.
We're half of what it is
we used to be.
The music stops
we're unable to hear
it.
Unable to sing it.
No we can't even
play it, or enjoy it.
Nothing is certain during
our time of loss.
We wake up each day
trying hard to figure it
all out.
How will we go on?
Will our lives ever mend
themselves?
Will we ever find solace
in the moon, sun, and
stars again?
Grief takes everything
away from us.
It's been such a long
time since I've danced.

Then early one spring
evening my sister brought
me new music Cowboy

Carter and my feet
remembered dancing.

cjj

Hues of Blue Tattooed on My Heart

All this time has passed, and I still look
for you in every sunrise and each calendar
month that circles the month of June.

I see your face in the memories of
our lives, as confetti speckled traces
of indigo hue stardust is left upon the
moon.

The years pass but I can't forget you.
Dear God, my heart won't let me.

cjj

Stargazing & Twirling Sparklers

Two little brown girls sat on
their porch gazing up at the sky
into the stars.
Wishing they had sparklers to
twirl and fireworks to celebrate
their independence too.
Sitting and wishing for a little
Holiday magic.
They sat on that porch staring
up at the sky for a very long time.
This year would be different not

mere spectators.

Fireworks arrived as if summoned
by wizard's magic.
But not just Fireworks
that balmy night in July.
Ice cream, candy, and soda pop too.
Two little brown girls were going to
Twirl sparklers and sound off very
loud poppers and fireworks for the

remainder of the night.
They were happy in that moment.
Creating memories as their mother
watched them celebrating
Independence Day from their front porch.

That day was epic and special.
A Day that would be remembered,

cherished and often spoken of.
Two little brown girls twirled sparklers

in their yard.
They ate ice cream with their mother
and stargazed up at the sky.

cjj

Unhealed Wounds

Robert Brooks, Marcellus Williams
Gone.
So many others like them with Black skin
Gone.
From Emmett Till to Trayvon Martin
all boys and men with Black skin
Gone.
Erik & Lyle Menendez have alabaster hued skin
Soon to be released from prison
on their way home.

cjj

Gun Violence

America has a problem with
Mass shootings and gun violence.
We experience it every day of our lives.
No knock warrants.
Stop and Frisk.
Routine Traffic Stops.
911 emergency calls for HELP.
What happens when the mass
Shooters and serial killers to show up
are the police?

cjj

Chapter Five
A Little Haiku

Early Risers

the market women
wearing very bright colors
greet us with a smile.

cjj

Flashing Hot

I can't stand the heat
so I'm leaving the kitchen
look for me outside.

cjj

Black Child Mortality

Since Emmett Till Black
children's lives have hung in doubt
Enough is Enough

cjj

Blood on Leaves

mine is the strange fruit
heritage hanging in trees
leaves splattered with blood.

cjj

Chapter Six
Feels & Thrills...

*"The elders have ceased from the gate,
the young men from their music."*

Life Changes

Cramps, bloating, pain,
mood swings.
Once a month we repeat.
Cramps, bloating, pain,
mood swings.
Our femininity is suddenly

thrown in flux.

During the middle years we
become shells of our former
selves.

Night sweats, hot flashes,
weight gain, thinning hair,
Insomnia, every night we
repeat.
Night sweats, hot flashes,
weight gain, thinning hair,
Insomnia.

No sleep.
Dear God, the customs of

womanhood is upon me.

cjj

Exhaustion

Exhausted as a Black woman
in Corporate America.
In motherhood.
In sisterhood.
In womanhood.
In business.
In cooking.
In cleaning.
In writing.
In shopping.
In living.
In dating.
In loving.
In marriage.
In church.
Out of church.
In driving.
In being.
In rearing children.
In teaching.
In Congress.
In Senate.
In politics.
In law.
In Menopause.
In counseling friends.
In friendship.
In fighting the good fight.
In standing my ground.

Overseas in Cannes,
can't they just let a Black
woman be?
Even in Paris on Red Carpets.
Shining my shine.
Exhausted.
Watching Parisian Security
in Cannes Disrespecting me.

cjj

Love to Love

We have loved to love.
Loved at our best
Loved at our worst.
Loved to fight,
Loved to make up.
Loved to date, marry,
and procreate.
Loved to build a life
Surpassed being lovers
Evolved to husband and
wife.
Loved through all the drama
Loved through all the tears.
Loved each other best all
these many years.
We have loved to love.

cjj

Onyx Blues

Melancholy has jumped on me,
wrestling me like the angel that
took hold of Jacob and wouldn't
let em' go.
My Blues are Onyx Blue.
How much more can I push down?
How much more am I expected to
forgive?
It's bubbling over, the rage is right
there on top of the surface.
Walking around carrying PTSD.
Waiting for it to show up outside
of me.
How would you feel, every few
weeks awaiting the next
Black fatality that becomes
the leading headline news article
and feature every day of your life?
Could be me, or someone I know.
May 3, 2024, Roger Forston a
23-year-old active-duty senior airman,
was fatally shot by a Florida sheriff's deputy.
Latest news headline.
I grab my chest and fall to my knees.
Ezra, my 23-year-old nephew same
age, same special ops unit, could be
the next daily news headline.
My Blues are Onyx Blue.

Cjj

Healing Rains

Stop breathing life into what you
have released.
Let it be, let it be.
I released my burdens the wind carried
them away to the sky.
The sky blew them beyond the heavens.
Even unto the third heaven.
God poured out his cleansing rain.
It eased my pain.
It healed my pain.
Now they lie buried deep within the heart
of the earth.
Release what you're holding on to
so you can be free.
God pours out his cleansing rain.
Let it be, let it be.

cjj

Up-tempo Grooves & Whirling Moves

The rhythm of the music
fills and takes over my
body as it filters in
every breathing space.
I can't control the
overwhelming pulse of
the up-tempo snare drum
or the strumming groove
of the bass.
I feel my body jerking in
perfect time now.
I'm propelled by the lindy hop
ancestors to take my whirling
feet to the synchronized
joyful dance floor.

cjj

God's People

Laughing, Dancing, Smiling.
Surviving
Creating Culture
History Maker's
Singing, Praying, Loving.
Trusting
Weary
Inventing
Finding a way
Resilient
You know them for they aren't like
any other nation within the whole
Earth.
Open your eyes and recognize these
wonderful, raven-colored people are
God's people.

cjj

Rushing

Rushing to catch fast moving
planes.
Rushing to wait on slow
Moving trains.
Rushing to power walk
through a mundane and
ordinary, routine life.
Perhaps one day I'll slow
down long enough to enjoy
the aroma of life's extraordinary
fragrant roses.

cjj

Onyx Eclipse at Noon

In this life people are a trip,
and I'm not talking vacation.
I'm speaking extreme envy
complete hateration.
Who does she think she is?
Gotta dis her
can't show love and support;
somehow that takes something
away from you.
That's why you gotta keep
your focus at all times
out here in these streets.
Knowing who you are
and where you're headed.
Move beyond the haters
limitations.
Move swiftly,
intently with purpose.
eclipsing the haters completely.
From eyes, lips, & yes
honey, fingertips.
There's nothing quite like an
onyx eclipse.
The sun and moon take a bow
at her presence.
She has it all together.
I'll be waiting and watching at
noon.
When that unmistakable onyx
shading of the sky turns down
all temperatures.

An untimely blotting out across
the sky results from the depths
of a rare, eclipsing mahogany soul.
Shading all the haters from eyes,
lips, and even fingertips.

cjj

Fury Poured Out

God is shaking the earth.
His wrath and anger kindled
much.
I say it very loudly he's
shaking the earth.
Right is wrong and wrong
made right.
The needy are hungry
living on the street day and
night.
Innocent blood stains the
street while wealthy people
in government feed their
insatiable greed
Wrath revealed from heaven
against all unrighteousness;
The state of the world is in
a constant mess.
People O People in the valley
of decision;
It's time for you to choose.
Do you remember the Creator's
mission?
At some point we must consider
Our maker.
With fury poured out the Lord
shall roar from Zion and the
heavens shall shake.
But the Lord is the hope of
the Children of Israel, them
he'll never forsake.
I say it very plainly,
God is shaking the earth.

cjj

Chapter Seven
Serenade At Dawn

"Then sang Moses and the children of Israel this song unto the Lord, and spake, saying, I will sing unto the Lord, for he hath triumphed gloriously: the horse and his rider hath he thrown into the sea."

Earth and Sky

All that's left is missing you.
There's no more joy, laughter.
No one to share my deepest
secrets, inadequacies, or
fears without judgement with.
You're not here to celebrate
my achievements or wins I
think that hurts most of all.
I cling to every memory and
pray they never start to fade.
There is earth and sky and
all the space in between.
Days upon days, weeks, and
now many long years of
missing my big brother.
They never tell us once the
brightest light stops shining
in our lives just how cold, the
darkness really becomes.
I clutch on to past memories of
you as if they are my only life
source.
What's left now is earth and sky
and many long years of missing
my big brother.

cjj

Cement Mixer Putty, Putty Sung by Dad

On sunny days
I hear my dad
Singing Slim
Gaillard.

I see him in every summer

garden and tropical flower.
As the sun beams
brightly on my face
I smile and say the
words:

Cement Mixer Putty, Putty.
Sunny days make me
think of dad and
I smile.
I can hear him humming,
singing those words
made famous by
Slim Gaillard and I
am suddenly transported home.

cjj

The Days of Youth

I remember the joy of youth.
Dancing all night till dawn.
Daylight beckoned tired and
aching feet quietly home.
Life was simpler somehow.
The days of dancing and
mirth have become hard and
cold.
These days there's no time
for dancing anymore.
Agility long gone.
Age has found me and
the demands on these
aching bones
and joints say most
assuredly girl, we have found
out we are now old.

cjj

God's Goodness

Each morning I awake
to hear the sweet sound
of the birds chirping.
I experience God's Goodness.
When his breath of life greets
me and I am on the wake up list,
I experience God's Goodness.
Every day my mobility is present
I experience God's Goodness.
The food he has provided, the
safe and warm sanctuary of home
are all tangible proofs of his goodness.
Days turn into nights health and
strength sustained.
A sound, strong, mind, able to thank
God for his Goodness.
Life brings forth many hard, uncertain,
and unknown circumstances.
In the early morning hours of each new day,
I am greeted by God's goodness, and I am
thankful.

cjj

Time for Dancing

Gotta get out of this blue funk.
Gotta get my Jhu jhu back and
put on some Mac Russian Red
Lips.
I don't live in down and out.
I want to cha cha and maybe
even Rumba or Samba.
Life is too short to allow sadness
to set up residence in my soul.
Look for me on the other side of
marvelous avenue.
Pack your bags Debbie Downer
you have over stayed your
welcome.
These sad times have got to go.
Gotta get out of this blue funk.
Gotta find my Jhu jhu fast.
I have to slip on those high heeled
shoes the color blue just never
really suited me.
Gotta paint this lifeless and
humdrum town chili pepper red.

cjj

Upside-down World

Love of everything other than God.
Seeking wealth.
Chasing death.
Wrong is right.
Peaceful makes you a prey.
No one prays.
Love of self but no one else.
Right is wrong.
Thieves take it all.
Impoverished in great lack.
Liars celebrated, promoted, and cheered.
Truth seekers strange and weird.
Honesty reviled.
Cheaters redeemed.
Virtue sneered.
This is the upside-down world we now
live in.
This place is not my home. I'm just passing through.
Upside-down world with wrong-side up views.
Catch me somewhere in the sphere when this
place becomes Right-side up again.
Hard to find me in the wreckage of this
Upside-down world.

cjj

Autumn Makes me Long for Summertime

We're headed for cooler temperatures
But I can't help but think about warmer
weather and happier times.
Summer and family reunions.
Now those were the best of times.
Seeing all your favorite relatives.
Especially the older ones.

No one hugged you like Aunt Laura.
Uncle Rudy dancing was our reunion
highlight.
He could move and out dance anyone
in the younger generation.

His body had a James Brown magic
and we all loved watching him dance.
There was Homemade ice cream with old
fashioned pound cake.

Everyone gathered around watching the
card games while the adults talked
much trash.

I remember family, celebrating our
origins and thankful that we could all
meet for a happy occasion.
There wasn't a safer time to party it
up and not feel guilty for eating way too
much of all the wrong things.

It wasn't illegal to drink spirits out in the open
then.

Uncle Thomas always drank way too much.
This always meant he and his wife were going
to give us kids an earful of PG 16 language.
She never let the poor guy get too loose.
Family reunions were a time for celebrating
lineage, bloodlines and family love.
Memories of summertime make me feel warm
and safe.

The Wallace clan had our share of real characters
but those family reunions were epic and adventurous.
Autumn makes me remember Uncle Rudy dancing
and I smile for a long while.

                                    cjj

Nature's Incubator

Spring makes my soul feel
alive.
The world wakes up and revives.
Everything is in bloom and warmer
Days that were shorter now are longer.
Newness of life
A time of wonder.
Renewal, Rebirth,
Rejuvenation, Resurrection.
The whole earth in bloom.
Springtime ultimately issues in
Summer.
Spring is the incubator and tide in
the earth where everything in nature is born anew.

cjj

Recollections of Ali in Autumn

Fall will always be our time.
Autumn aromas saturate
the air infusing all the spices
we love to inhale.
Ginger, nutmeg, and an extra
splash of cinnamon invites us
to our favorite Fall meeting
space.
French styled outdoor cafés and
Chai Tea Lattes.
We never minded the cooler
temperatures.
Warm embraces and scandalous
Secrets shared between me and you.
I loved your big smile and wavy
Dark brown curly hair.
Each Autumn I think of you.
Such a loyal friend you were,
honest and true.
The inside jokes that only we knew.
Thick as thieves, me and you.
As familiar as Autumn colored
leaves:
Red, Burnt Orange, and yellow covering
the ground.
Fall was our time to just chill and be.
Stolen time away as if we willed it to stand
still only for us.
Each Autumn I think of my friend Ali.
We needed those breaks in our days
to make certain life was settled that
we would be okay.

You will always be a treasured recollection my favorite Fall memory.
Each Autumn I recall spiced scents we loved.
I always think of you.
Fall is a time for tasty warm drinks, cozy embraces, and shared conversations the heart won't let us ever forget.

cjj

25 Sunrises of Cognac Colored Eyes

It never gets old drifting
off to sleep in *Dark Gable's*
slender arms.
I never tire of having you
sleep by my side.
I have watched 26 sunrises
with you for 24 years and
each morning it's as new
as seeing our very first one.
I stare into loving eyes the
color of the most poised and
refined cognac, and think
to myself there isn't a finer
Black man to ever walk
this earth.

cjj

Chapter Eight
Cornerstone Compositions

"And when they had sung a hymn,
they went out into the mount of olives."

Moonchild (Lyris' Poem)

Hello, round-faced girl with the prickly hair.

You are my greatest joy.

When I think of you, a thousand perfectly shaped moons
come to mind.

I am recalling your smile.

Lighting up my life, just like the moon illuminates a dark
and somber sky.

You're a very old soul. Your wisdom far exceeds your
years.

Tell me, have you been here before?

We are extended selves sharing in joy, feeling each
other's pain.

You are my heart's delight.

You are one perfectly shaped moon illuminating my life.

cjj

Leave Me Alone with My Blues

Some days, all a person has is
    their blues.
I'm talking the
    Albert King
I've-Been-Down-Since-I-Began-
    to-Crawl
        blues.
The down home,
Play-the-Other-Record or Two-
    collard-greens-with-cornbread-
on-the-side
        blues.
The kind where you just want
    to be left alone with your
melancholy. Let me feel
    what I'm feeling.
The pain of living Black
    struggle, plantation
        blues.

I've-been-up-all-night, -ain't-nothin'-

    going-right, BB-King-and-Lucille-

I-Think-You-Made-Your-Move-

    Too-Soon

        blues.

I'm in a Z.Z. Hill

    frame of mind.

Just leave me alone with my

    down home

        blues.

Let-the-somber-and-

    pensive-gloom-of-my-

soul-loop-on-constant-

    repeat-

until-its-familiar-cadence-

    becomes- "Stormy-Monday"

        blues.

Remembering Sylvester while

    listening to T-Bone Walker.

              cjj

Forgotten Zion Melodies

Mary and Martha have every reason to
weep and moan...
Black souls have borne witness to the following
atrocities on North American shores:
The Auction blocks of Jamestown paraded my
raped and mutilated children.
Founding fathers' Southern Slave plantations
and cotton fields, Jim Crow, Segregation,
Night rides of the Ku Klux Klan,
Selma Alabama,
Church Bombings,
Bloody Sunday and Edmund Pettus Bridge.
Tulsa Oklahoma-Black Wallstreet,
Lynchings and unarmed civilian shootings at
the hands of White police.
Civil rights, and voting rights violations,
Whitewashing of Black History and Black
Literature, Book Bans,
corrupt politicians,
Least in wealth doubled in illness
Tripled in violence and death.
My weary Black soul has long forgotten the
comforting lulls of the ancestors.
I lie awake at 4:40 a.m. with full knowledge there
is no safe space for Black women/people
there simply never was.
Not on this blood-soaked soil. Not on these shores.
I long to hear my children singing their lost
Zion melodies.

Wishing I could forget Antebellum rhapsodies.
So tired of singing slave master songs,
will we ever break free of founding fathers' wrongs???
Daring to recount, tell, and write my Black History at
this time is what makes the Black writer Brave.
A daughter of Zion, a royal priesthood. So much more
than descendants of former slaves.

cjj

Vagabond Blues

Living like a daughter of Cain
Disinherited without promise.
Remembering the land of
milk and honey but can't sing
my ancestor's song,
the song of Moses.
I sit a stranger cast off in a
strange land.
Longing to return to our
hallowed promised land.
Can't escape this speckled bird
heritage worn upon my back
Disowned, own my own,
living like a cast away,
hurting now, a wretched
vagabond.
Left for a prey, a sign and wonder,
there's no escaping that.
The curses poured out upon
me living life in complete lack.

Afflicted the Job of my

generation.

Fury poured out

longing for home scattered

waiting complete restoration.

Living as a captive least among

the nations.

cjj

Evolution of the Blues

I am old, dirt roads.

I am soul.

I am cotton gins,

and Mississippi

cotton fields.

The daughter of a

a sharecropper that

sang plantation songs.

Daddy partied with his

Old Grand Dad Whiskey

in hand, all night long.

You could find him in the

Juke Joint but he worked

double hard.

Meaner than any old,

abandoned, Junkyard dog.

I am negro spirituals.

I am Jim Crow

I am the origins of

Little Richard, Chuck Berry

and *Fats Domino.*

The heart and soul of

Good time music

rightfully named *Rock 'N' Roll.*

I am corn bread

and collard greens.

Fried chicken too.

The daughter of a *BLUES MAN*

who lived *Cheating-in-the-*

Next-Room.

I witnessed the birth of

honky-tonk and *ragtime.*

I am shouts and chants;

Lost *Canaan Ballads* howled

upon the moon.

The birth of soulful *blue grass,*

I AM THE EVOLUTION OF THE BLUES.

cjj

Chapter Nine
Lyrics by Moonlight

"Hear, O ye kings; give ear, O ye princes;
I, even I, will sing unto the Lord;
I will sing praises to the Lord God of Israel."

Strangers in a Strange Land

Boy, Gal,
Spade
Spook
Every few decades
Our people renamed.
Negro
Colored, Black
Address us by our names.
Presidents
First ladies
Supreme Court justices
The hate remains the same.
Senators,
Congressional legislators
Address us by our names.
Educators, Entertainers,
Athletes, Scientists,
Black plight still unchanged
Strangers in a strange land
Address us by our names.
We're the children of Israel
Driven from our homelands
crossing many seas.
Degraded left for a stain
Placed in servitude
Bought and sold
Address us by our names.
Every couple of decades
as the seasons change
Our people renamed.

No matter what we accomplish
Black plight remains the same.
Doctors,

Lawyers
Linguists
Historians
Novelists, Poets, Authors
Address us by our names.
Strangers in a strange land
I must insist you address us by
our name.

cjj

Caramel Apples & Goldfinches

Autumn leaves
Red, yellow, and
Orange colored trees.
Change of seasons
brings a much cooler
breeze.
Pumpkins and spices
Crops are gathered in,
Fall is the time for
meeting with friends.
Goldfinches and Robins
rest upon weather beaten
decks.
Chilling temperatures
result in scarves upon
cold, sensitive, necks.
Carmel apples and
Vibrant mums,
usher in a full Fall
moon our season
of reaping Autumn
harvest fun.

cjj

Hollow

She fed me.
She clothed me.
She nurtured me.
She loved me.
She was history,
strength and honor.
She cared for me.
She was my identity.
She prayed, championed
and advocated for me.
She was strong for me.
She took on wrong and
defined right for me.
She healed me.
She saw me.
She was me.
She was kind to me.
She was lineage, and culture.
The one that protected and
believed in me.
She was my mother.
The woman I aspired to be.
My heart's first love.
Where she led I always
followed.
She gave me the God of
my Hebrew father's.
Life doesn't prepare us
for such crushing final
goodbyes.
Tears find me hollow
weeping silently late into
the night.

cjj

Unbroken

The middle passage couldn't break us.
Chains and slave ships couldn't break us.
Disease and Sickness couldn't break us.
Auction blocks couldn't break us.
Hatred couldn't break us.
Triple K Night rides, hoods and sheets
burning
crosses across American soil couldn't
break us.
Jim Crow couldn't break us.
Lynchings couldn't break us.
Segregation and poll taxation couldn't
break us.
Police brutality misuse of tasers and night
sticks/batons couldn't break us.
Strength made us.
God covers us.
Light surrounds us.
Love empowers us.
Joy is found within us.
We are a wondrous people.
There are no limitations of
what God can do for us.
People of the sun we are most
SPLENDOROUS.

cjj

Qaadir and Naazir

Double blessings
Twin boys born
Socialized in
mama's womb.
Double joy
Double love
Double trouble
Twin boys forever
Silenced.
Without Reason.
A mountain top
became twin boys
tomb.
19 years old
mama now mourns
Beautiful Twin boys
Double blessings
tragically gone.

cjj

America has proven they're incapable of protecting
Black men/boys from the greatest terror known to them
unlawful racist police.

Melanin Enchantments

Fill up the sum Black child
Bridge every gap.
Make your presence known
leave nothing to question.
In every space let them know
you were there.
That melanin capability
many refer to as magic
let its presence be felt
everywhere.
Go where they tell you
you, can't go.
Show up in that space
that is where you belong
for sure.
Fill up the sum Black child
Bridge every gap.
There is nothing like
Melanin capability always
trust and believe that.
Betting on Black cause that's
where the magic's at.

cjj

Begin Again Tomorrow

Sometimes we get to a
place and space in life
where it's all just bad.
We can't see an end out
of sorrow.
Pain is present like
sandpaper in our lives.
It's just as abrasive and rough.
We seek relief but can't find it.
Wanting the pain to end.
Wanting the suffering to end.
Wanting the hurt and confusion to end.
Needing to be happy again.
Wanting the sorrow to end.
Wanting the bad part of living to end.
Hopeful for tomorrow a new day.
Maybe happiness can be found tomorrow.
A new day it will be for me.
Maybe I can begin again then.
Maybe happiness is waiting for me
somewhere in tomorrow.

cjj

Beyond Deferred Dreams

What's really out there beyond
deferred dreams?
When we acquire what we
really want does it even matter?
Does anyone know?
Can they tell us the rest of life's
answers?
Is anything certain?
Is anything sure?
What's really out there beyond
deferred dreams?
Is happiness even possible
what does it feel like?
What does any of it mean?
As Langston and Edgar once
said, when all is acquired in life,
that we see or seem, it's yet but
a dream within a deferred dream.

cjj

The Poets Shine

The poets lay their emotions bare.

Putting our social consciences on

the line.

We write it how we see it

live it.

No allegiance in our politics.

Neither Republican nor Democrat

A rat rather red or blue is still a rat.

Poets write their words, thoughts,

and sentiments.

Sometimes written with and without

many resentments.

Line by line, in perfect and imperfect

rhythm we rhyme.

Using metaphors, similes, and our

hearts we write.

Fueled by God's goodness and light

the poets write, the poets write.

We view the world around us laying

our emotions bare.

The poets are seen and heard everywhere.

We write it how we see it we write our

words how we have lived it.

In dawn's waning hours and morning's

first light

the poets write, the poets write

cjj

Stumbling Backwards

No one hugged like mom.
Cooked like mom.
Baked like mom.
Praised you or prayed for
you like mom.
Laughed like mom,
Enjoyed life like mom.
Her embrace was the
warmest and safest place
in the world and under the

sun.
When she championed for
you there was no way you
weren't going to win.
No one was smarter than
mom.
Not even dad with all those
degrees.
No one was like our mother.
We loved her like we loved
no other.
She was warmth and light
and now that she's gone
we're having to figure it out
all on our own.
Stumbling backwards through
this lackluster life.

cjj

Cornrows

More than a hairstyle.
A lifeline.
A Message.
Each braid states its own story.
Tribal identification.
Your age. Your status.
Intricate patterns were
living symbols of identity.
During the North Atlantic
slave trade secret escape maps
were concealed and braided
right within the hair.
Cornrows guided paths to freedom.
Survival, Resistance, Belief.
Seeds were sometimes hidden
within the braids too.
Tiny grains of hope.
Seeds of SURVIVAL.
A necessary lifeline.
Providing food and sustenance
for dangerous unknown
journeys ahead.
Now imagine carrying survival
and escape routes right on your
head!
Resistance.
Cornrows were strategic
styled silent REBELLION.
Every braid a masterful
symbol of FAITH, DEFIANCE and
POWER.

This is our history and
culture.
A legacy of Defiance and
Strength.
Bo Derek can never replace
Such majestic Black Confidence.
She never lived our rebellious
historical story.
Only appropriated our soulful
melanated regal glory.
Now tell me again, who's the real
original and only ten?

cjj

Chapter Ten
Psalms At Sunrise

*"I will sing of mercy and judgement:
unto thee, O Lord, will I sing."*

The Light Bearer

A slip of a woman influenced many Black
writers that our words matter.
She single handedly lit the fuse.
It wasn't that she was saying something
new but she spoke it how we did.
In our rhythm. In our vernacular.
The language was raw in your face
without apology and not requiring
anyone's permission.
She knew that we knew, that she was FIRE.
Above it all in every way.
We wanted to be her.
She was representation for us.
Strength, honor, encouraging Black writers
to release our thoughts, words and dialog into
the firmament.
Set it ablaze and burn it all down if you have to.

She was revolution and made us think we could
be that too.
Many of us listened to her words.
We're sad today because part of us is missing.
Look up brotha, look up sistah.
Her presence is in the air. I can see and feel Nikki
Everywhere.
Her essence is in the wind, air, and rain.
The rap beats that we repeat and dance to.
Nikki was our mirror our proximity to necessary
and unforgettable truths.

She's in every sparkling rain drop, and every new

moon.
Nikki's my reason to jazz loud in June.
She's my reason to write and seek solace
where light gathers causing words to take flight.
Nikki was the light bearer. A reflective luminescent
source of literary light.
Her poetry is the rebirth and retelling of Black history,

Black culture and Black Literature.

I read Nikki's poems, and I am reborn.

cjj

N'awlins Jazz Piping

Fish frying
Oil hot popping
all over the stove
top popping on me.
Satchmo piping
lively N'awlins Jazz
Wild, untamed and
free.
Night comes on slowly
Ebony like me.
Jazz playing loudly
just like daddy played.
My feet mimic their
upbeat Rhythm.

I repeat
what I think I heard
Satchmo say.
Jasmine vines calling
my name.
While fish crackles loud
in the well-used frying
pan.
Enjoying Satchmo
singing fills my heart
with glee.
Nightfall claiming the
dusky eventide.
Sun below the horizon
Night comes in slowly,

Night comes in gently,

for all the world to see.
Quietly, Onyx fell on
nightfall Black Like me.

                    cjj

Blackbird Simone

Confident
Courageous
Gifted
Talented
Strong
Rebel
Intelligent
Activism
Civil and Women's rights
Conscience
Nina Simone was WOKE long before the word

was ever born.
Nina set and determined a Black woman's
worth.
She referred to herself as a Rebel with
a cause.
Standing ovations performing in
Europe receiving White and Black applause.
No one caressed or delivered life and
breath to a lyric like Nina did.
Celebrating Black culture honoring
ethnicity she was Women's Lib.
I think about Nina and all that she
left behind proclaiming her greatness
today,
Nina Simone a woman to be remembered
for all of time.

A woman who lived an extraordinary life.

Nina Simone enchanted a nation here and abroad.
When Nina sang to us, we felt the presence
of God.

Known to the rest of the world as Nina Simone but
for my dad and I she will always be our little girl
blue.

Our divine Blackbird soaring in and beyond the sky;
a woman to be remembered for all of time.
When that distinct crackling of the needle meets
vinyl: I hear Nina's bluesy Contralto textures
& tones, and I still experience the presence of
God.

cjj

Peace!

*"And they sung as it were a new song
before the throne, and before
the four beasts, and the elders:
and no man could learn that song but
the hundred and forty and four thousand
which were redeemed from the earth."*

Author Bio

Chyrel J. Jackson is a 2025 Poet Laureate, award winning author, and #1 Ranked Best Selling Amazon Author. Reared and raised in the South Suburbs outside Chicago. African American Literature influenced her writing and is one of her favorite genres. Chyrel Jackson writes in the spirit of her past great Literary ancestors. 2021 garnered Chyrel her very first literary nomination, Pushcart Nominee-Poem "Love Unspoken," Published in *Heart Beats Anthology*.

The Summer of 2022 Chyrel was a contributing writer in the #1 Best Seller ranked Anthology *Not Just Anybody Can Be Dad*.

Along with her sister, Lyris D. Wallace, they published *SistersRoc'N'Rhyme Presents Poems in the Key of Life*, *Mirrored Images* and *Different Sides of the Same Coin*. This edgy writing duo appears in multiple published poetry Anthologies, Literary Journals, and International Global Magazines. You will find them always writing. Creating written legacies one book at a time.

Chyrel J. Jackson is one writer that has found her poetic voice.

You can find her on:

SISTERSROCNRHYME.BLOGSPOT.COM and **linktr.ee/ChyrelJ_Jackson66**

Previously Published Poetry Collections

SistersRoc'N'Rhyme Presents Poems in the Key of Life

Mirrored Images

Different Sides of the Same Coin

Poetry & Prose Poetry Journal

Genesis of the Scribe Poetry Journal

Featured in numerous poetry anthologies and literary publications/journals, & Global Magazine

Book Club Discussion Questions:

1. How did the cover assist your understanding of the book's subject?
2. Would you prefer this standard-sized collection or a smaller-sized book such as a chapbook about the same theme? Please elaborate.
3. The title "Unsung Canaan Ballads" has a specific meaning. What does the title mean to you? How is this theme meaningful to you?
4. Did scripture texts spring forth during your poem readings? Please discuss how they are significant to you.
5. Which poems stood out to you? Please elaborate on the significance of these poems.
6. What is the important parallel between the Civil Rights movement and Black Literature? How did you see this parallel within this collection?
7. Why is it important to have diverse writers in literature?
8. Where did the author grow up? How is this significant to this collection?
9. What key takeaway did the book provide for you?
10. If you could ask the author a question, what would you ask?

11. What tunes or musical styles does this book evoke?

12. How original/unique was this book?

13. What Black writer had the greatest influence on the author? What are your thoughts about this influential writer?

14. Did reading this collection inspire you to read more Black writers? If so, whose works are you interested in reading?

15. If you are a poet or other type of writer, did this book inspire further reading or writing for you? Please elaborate.

16. Would you consider exploring further works penned by this author? What influenced this decision?

www.ingramcontent.com/pod-product-compliance
Lightning Source LLC
Chambersburg PA
CBHW020356130626
46549CB00006B/2300